Rock Pool Secrets

Narelle Oliver

Down on the rocky shore,
waves crash and smash.
Then the tide goes out and the sea is calm.
It's a good time to explore rock pools.

At first glance there's nothing much to see.
But the rock pools are full of secrets.

Nestled between the rocks are anemones.
Like flowers with sticky tentacles
they grasp and tug and cling.

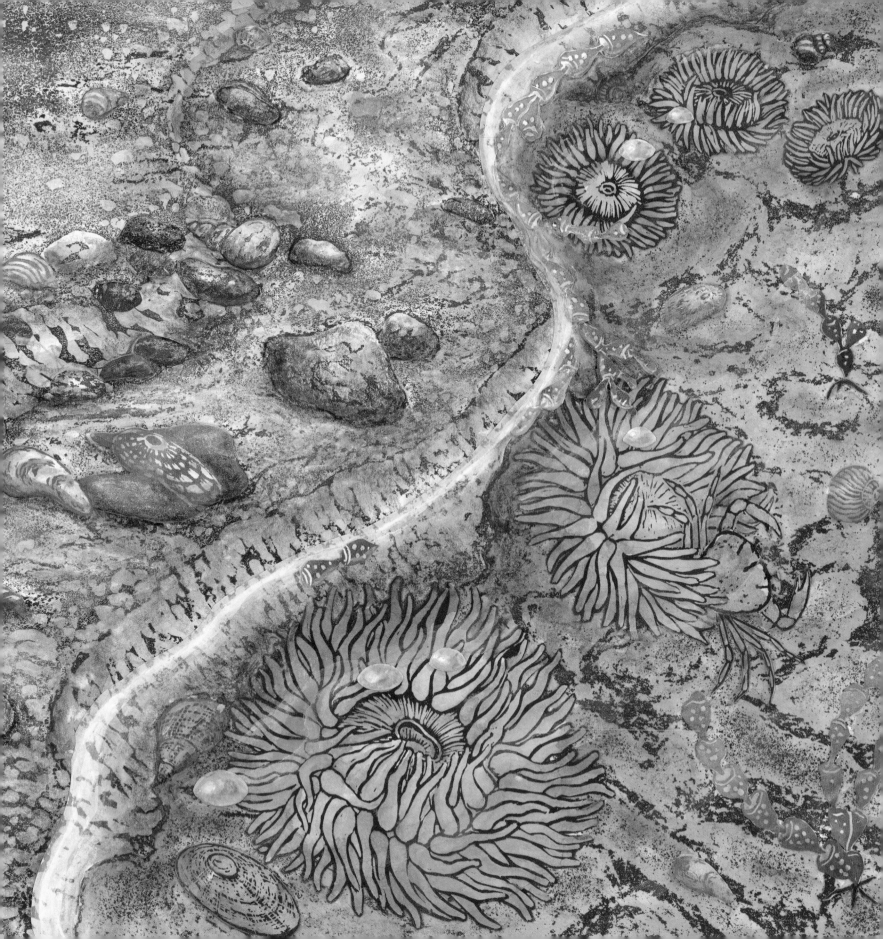

Empty shells are everywhere.
Once there were soft mollusc bodies
inside them – they are gone now.
But something is curled
up and hiding…

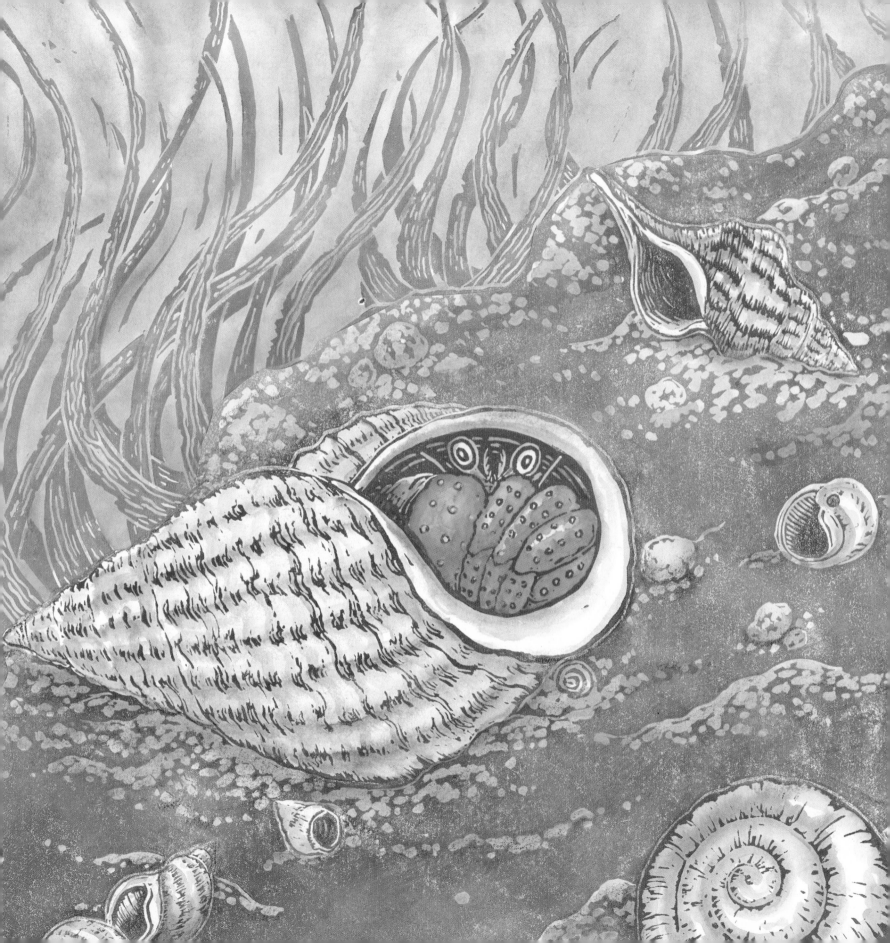

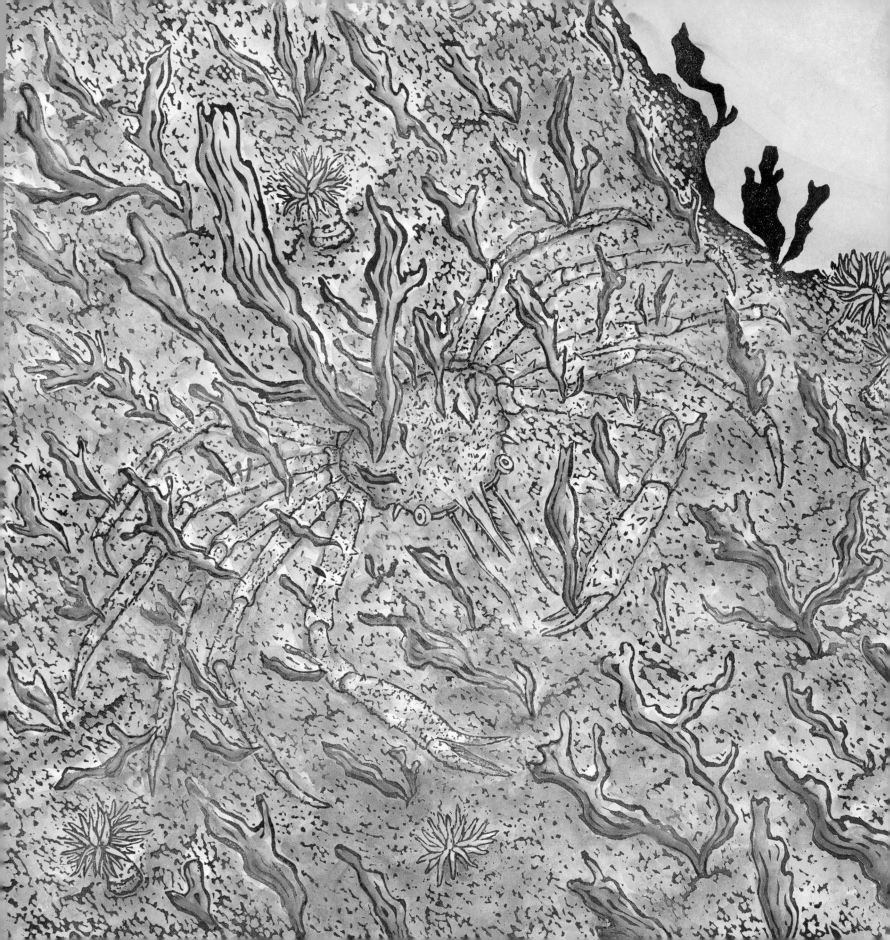

Not all rock pool crabs hide in shells.
Can you see the decorator crab?
It disappears by disguising itself.
Carefully, the crab uses its claws
to stick seaweed pieces on
little hooks and spikes.
Soon it looks like the rocks
and weeds around it.
Then the crab keeps still.

Deeper down in the rock pool
something shoots like a rocket
into tangles of seaweed.

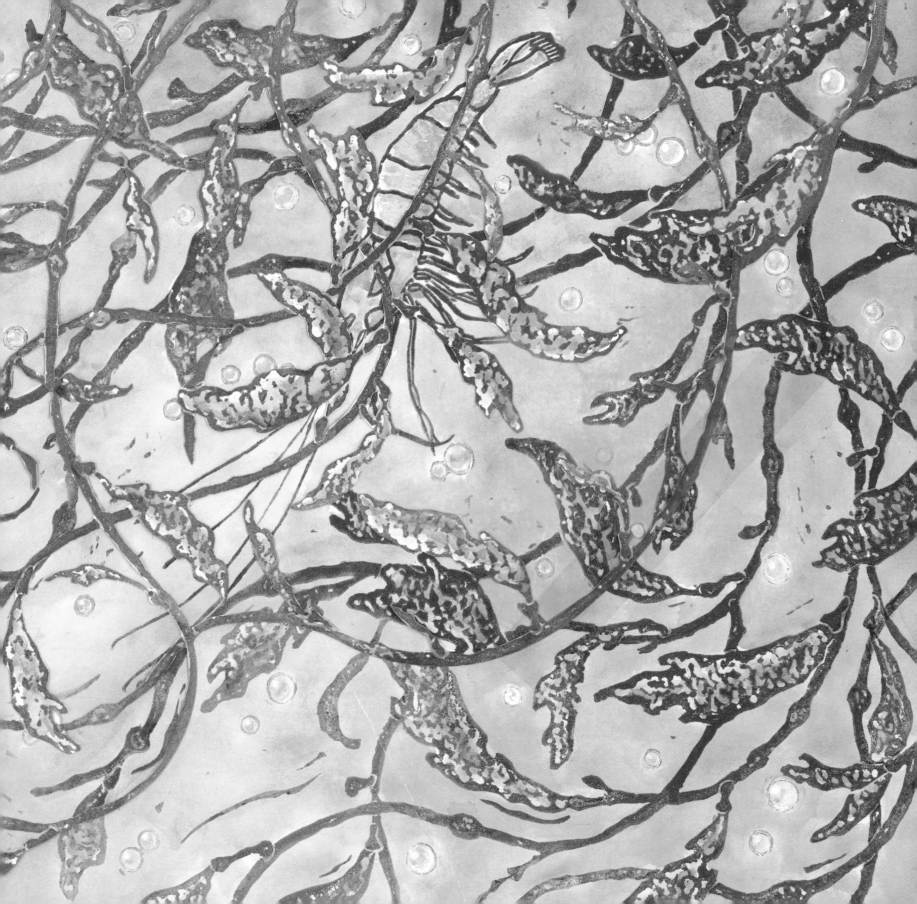

Holes and crevices in rocks
make good secret places too.
Speckled eyes peep from a miniature cave.
A tiny shrimp floats by
and does not notice.

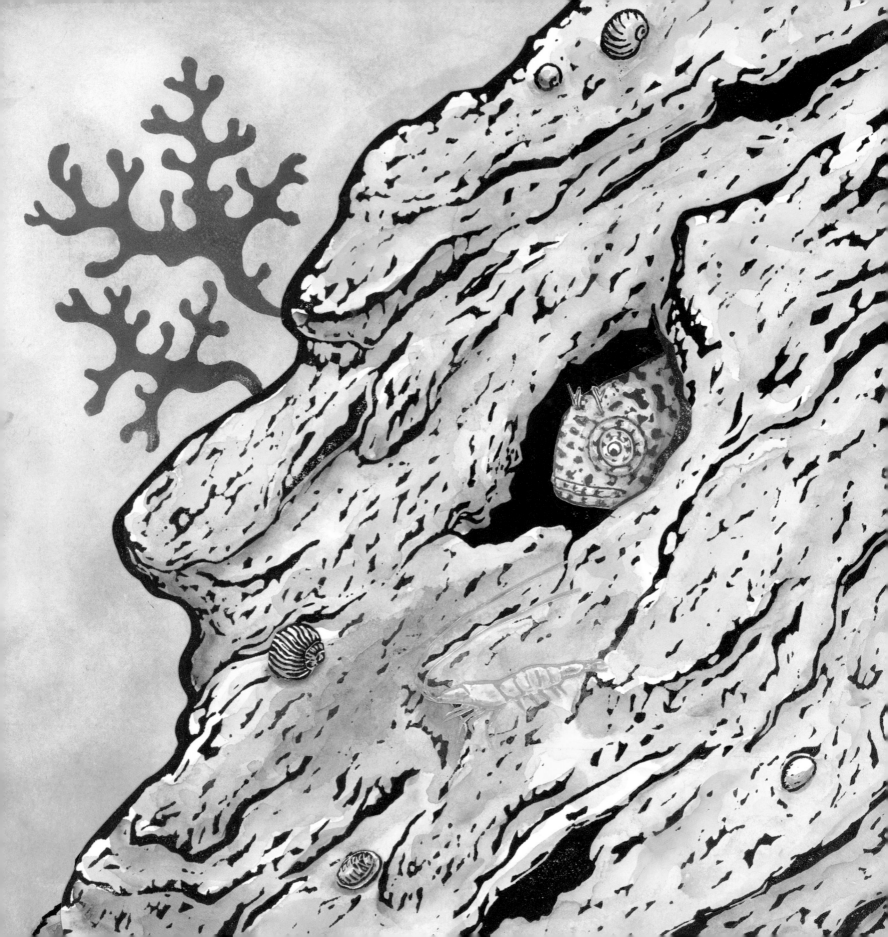

This starfish doesn't need a hole to hide in.
It looks just like the rock.
Can you find it?
Lots of suction-cup feet cement its bumpy
body to the surface
and when the starfish moves,
its suction feet shuffle very slowly.

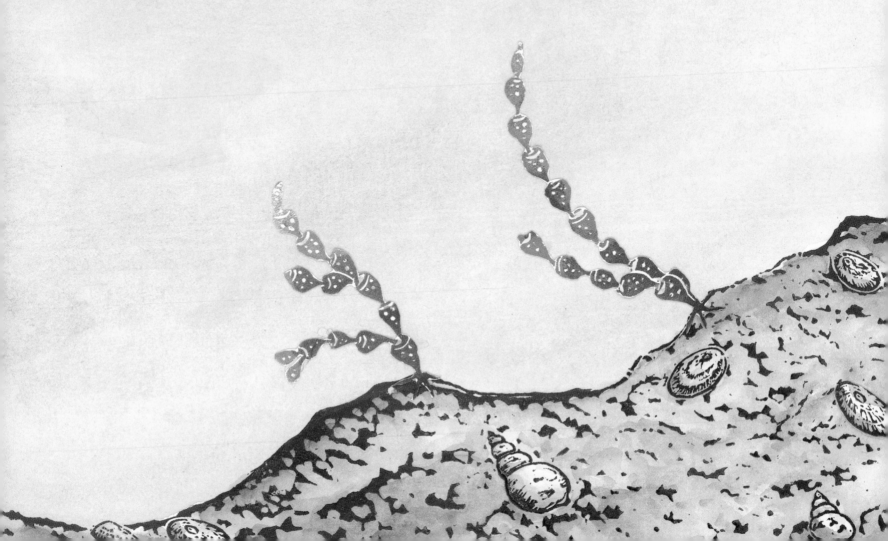

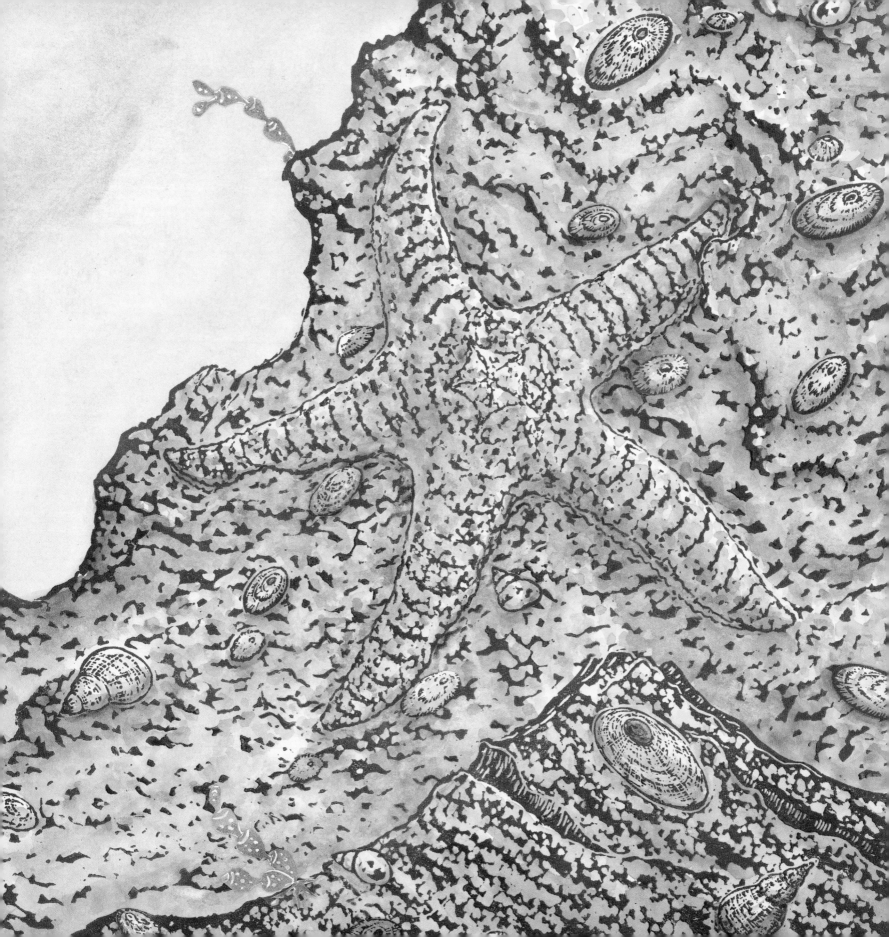

Whoosh!
An ink jet streams into the water
and makes a swirling cloud.
Something has disappeared
in the patch of darkness.

There's no inky cloud to hide the sea slug.
Its blobby body melts into the rock's shape
and its frilly top sways with the weed.
The mottled sea slug fits right in.
Can you see its outline?

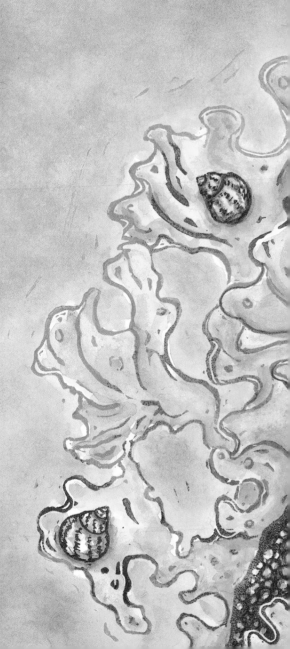

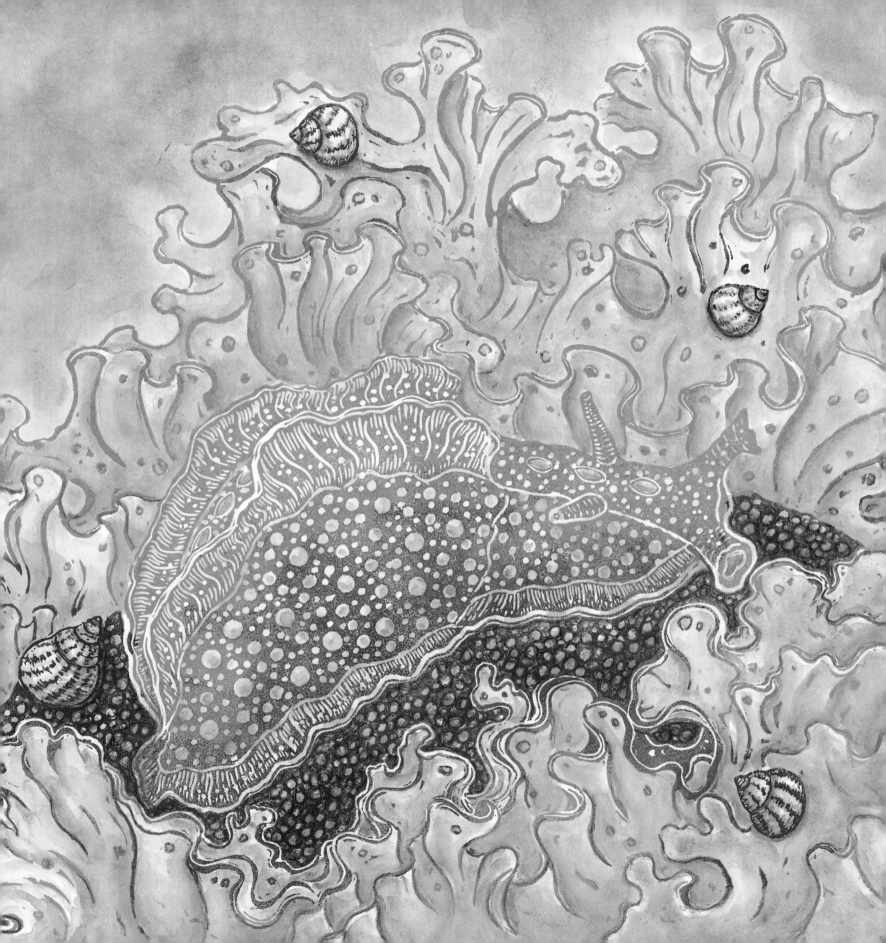

Out on the rock pool edge,
sea snails lie still in the sun.
To keep moist and safe, their shells
are shut tight – sealed
with special lids.

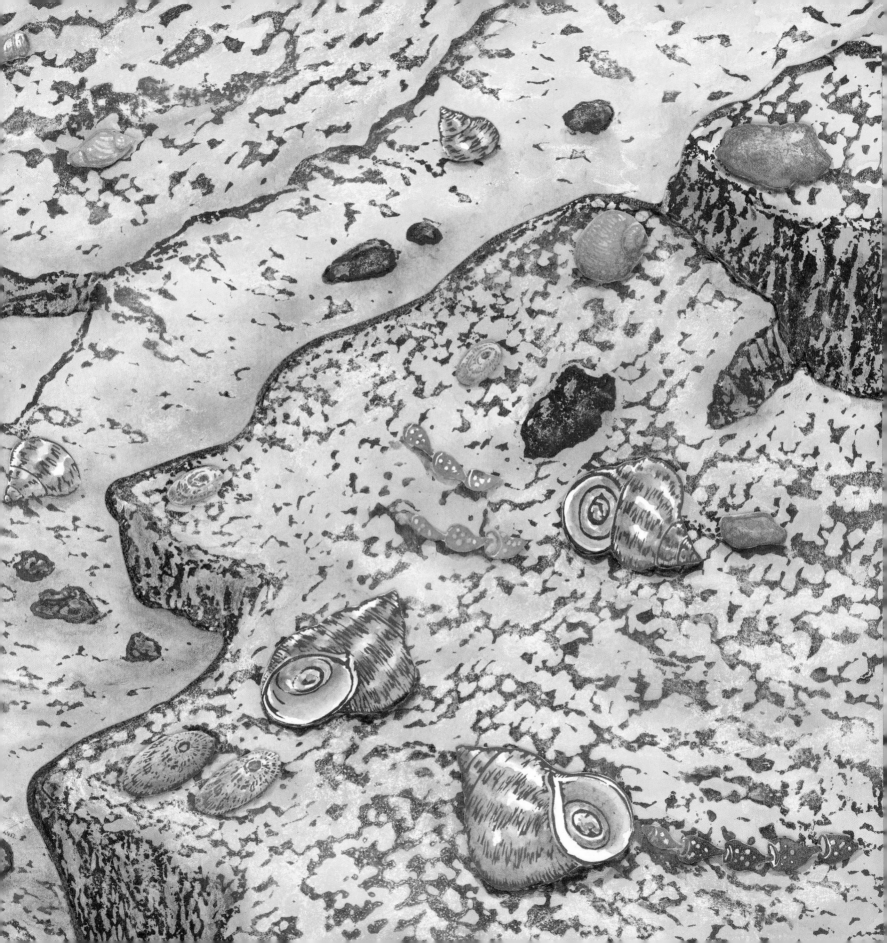

Minute by minute, the
tide creeps higher.
The rock pool becomes
deeper and wider.
But there's still time…

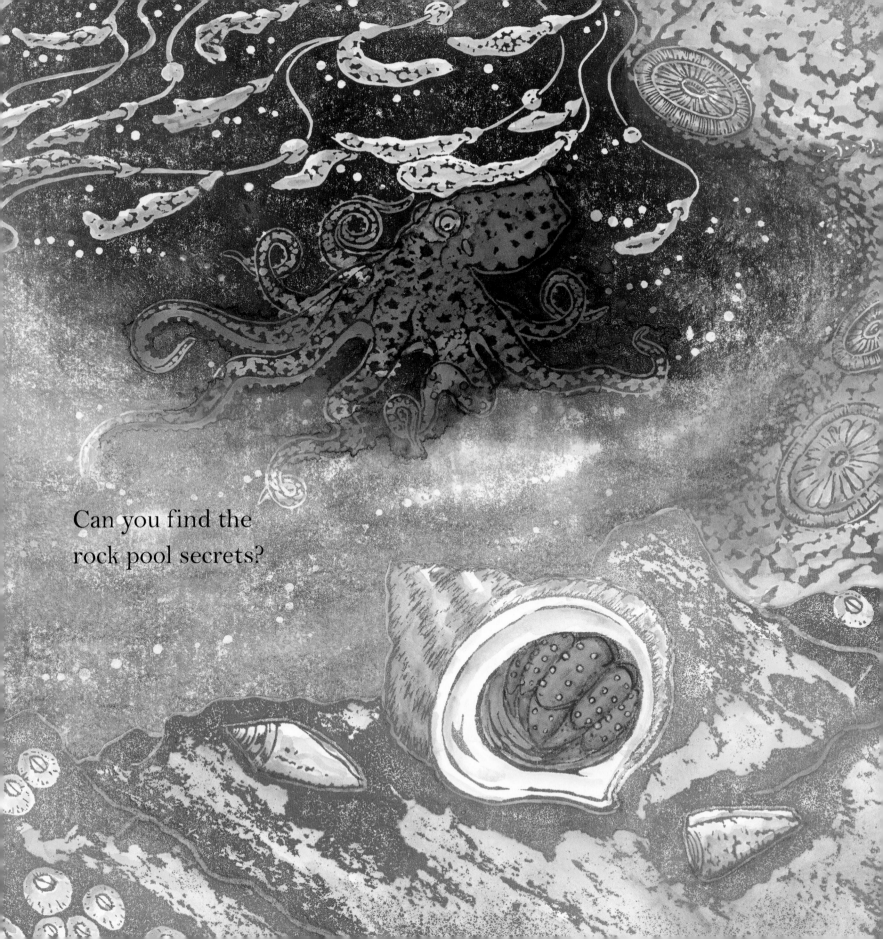

Can you find the
rock pool secrets?

Why do rock pools have secrets?

There are lots of reasons rock pool creatures may be difficult to see at first glance. Some are hiding from other animals. Others are sheltering from the crashing waves. They might jam themselves between rocks or take cover in little caves or in deeper rock pools where the waves cannot reach so easily. Some nestle in thick cushions of seaweed and go with the flow.

High shallow rock pools may escape the bashing waves, but they can become too hot or too cold or too salty or not salty enough for many rock pool creatures.

So most of them go deeper – which means you have to wait until low tide to see them!

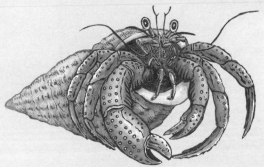

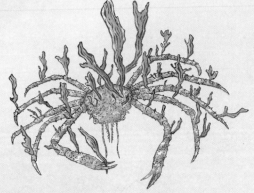

Sea anemone

The sea anemone's tentacles grip and sting any rock pool creature that touches them, then they pull it into its mouth – the opening in the middle of the tentacles.

Hermit crab

Unlike other crabs, most hermit crabs have a long soft bottom that curls around inside an empty sea snail shell. This bottom has a special tip that sticks to the inside of the shell.

Decorator crab

Most decorator crabs disguise themselves with pieces of seaweed. Some go a step further and stick poisonous anemones onto the tops of their shells to keep predators away.

Shrimp

The shrimp swims using five pairs of "swimmerets". They look like short hairy legs but are actually little paddles. When frightened, the shrimp can dart backwards using its tail.

Goby fish

Not all gobies eat shrimp. The "burrowing shrimp" digs a sand hole to share with the "watchman goby". In return, the better-sighted goby warns the shrimp of danger as it dashes into the hole.

Starfish

The suction-cup feet of the starfish are not just for clinging and shuffling. Some of these feet can smell prey. The starfish has eyespots on the end of each arm.

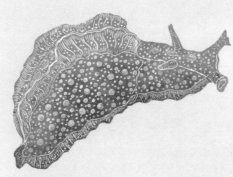

Octopus

Apart from shooting out an inky cloud, many octopuses hide by blending in with what is around them or squeezing into narrow places. Some can instantly change to bright colours to scare predators.

Sea slug

With no shell for protection, some sea slugs rely on camouflage. Greenish sea slugs can get their colour from the algae they eat, which helps them to match their algae-covered surroundings.

Sea snail

A special bump on the sea snail's squishy body makes a chalky liquid, which turns hard to form its shell. A different part of its body makes the lid. The sea snail adds to both as it grows.